Three Pampered Pugs

Pet Day at School

by Sandra Kitabjian

Illustrated by Karine Makartichan

Copyright © 2020 by Sandra Kitabjian

All rights reserved. No part of this book may be used or reproduced in any manner whatsoever without the express written permission of the publisher.

ISBN 978-0-578-74338-7

Three Pampered Pugs – Pet Day at School
Book and cover design by Sose Bejian
Illustrations by Karine Makartichan

First edition, 2020

Three Pampered Pugs@threepamperedpugs

Featuring...

 Khasi

 Sister Emma

 Kash

 Khloe

 Leah

 Rocco

 Talia

 Noelle

 Cameron

With special thanks to

Linda Ammazzaorsi, Sose Bejian, Mary Burns and Karen Sookiasian

"It's time to wake up,"
Mom said to each one,
"I promise today, will be lots of fun."

"We have somewhere to go,
I can hardly wait,
but we must hurry up,
and we shouldn't be late."

Down the stairs they did run,
and outside they would go,
where they'd take care of their business,
as you would know.

**Then into the kitchen,
this cute little brood,
ran straight to their bowls,
where they gobbled their food.**

"It's Pet Day at school,
so you need to get dressed,
I want to be sure that you all look your best."

Mom primped them and preened them,
from head to toe;
the three pampered pugs
were now ready to go.

She lifted each one
into the car,
and buckled them in,
the ride wasn't too far.

The pugs were all squealing
and squirming around,
Mom said to the three,
"Please try to calm down."

She reminded them
that they must try to be good,
to remember their manners,
the way charming pugs should.

They arrived at the school,
in no time flat,
went straight to the playground
where the three of them sat.

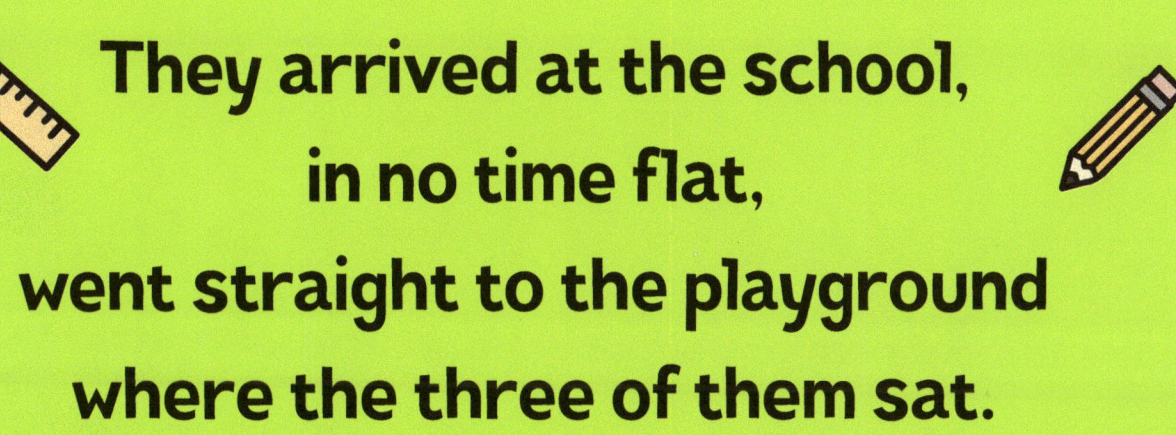

There were all sorts of pets
that showed up for pet day,
but none quite as adorable as the pugs,
I must say.

All of a sudden,
they heard a strange noise,
rushing towards them were
the girls and boys.

The children all giggled
with delight to see,
the three darling pugs
sitting under a tree.

With curly tails wagging,
the sweet little pugs,
were greeted by all
with kisses and hugs.

After some time
mom said to the bunch,
"It's time to get going,
you must have your lunch."

**She lifted each one
back into the car,
and buckled them in,
the ride wasn't too far.**

Once they got home,
outside they would go,
where they'd take care of their business,
as you would know.

Then into the kitchen on quick little feet,
They ran straight to the table
for something to eat.

When they were finished,
mom took out a wipe,
cleaned all three faces
with one quick swipe.

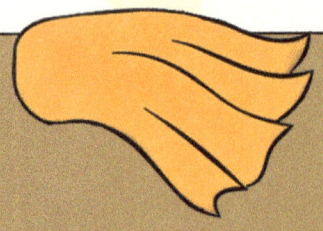

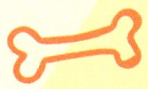

The pugs were exhausted,
from all the day's fun.
They climbed onto their bed,
one-by-one.

zzzZ

In no time at all,
they were snoring away,
dreaming of the fun
that they had at Pet Day.

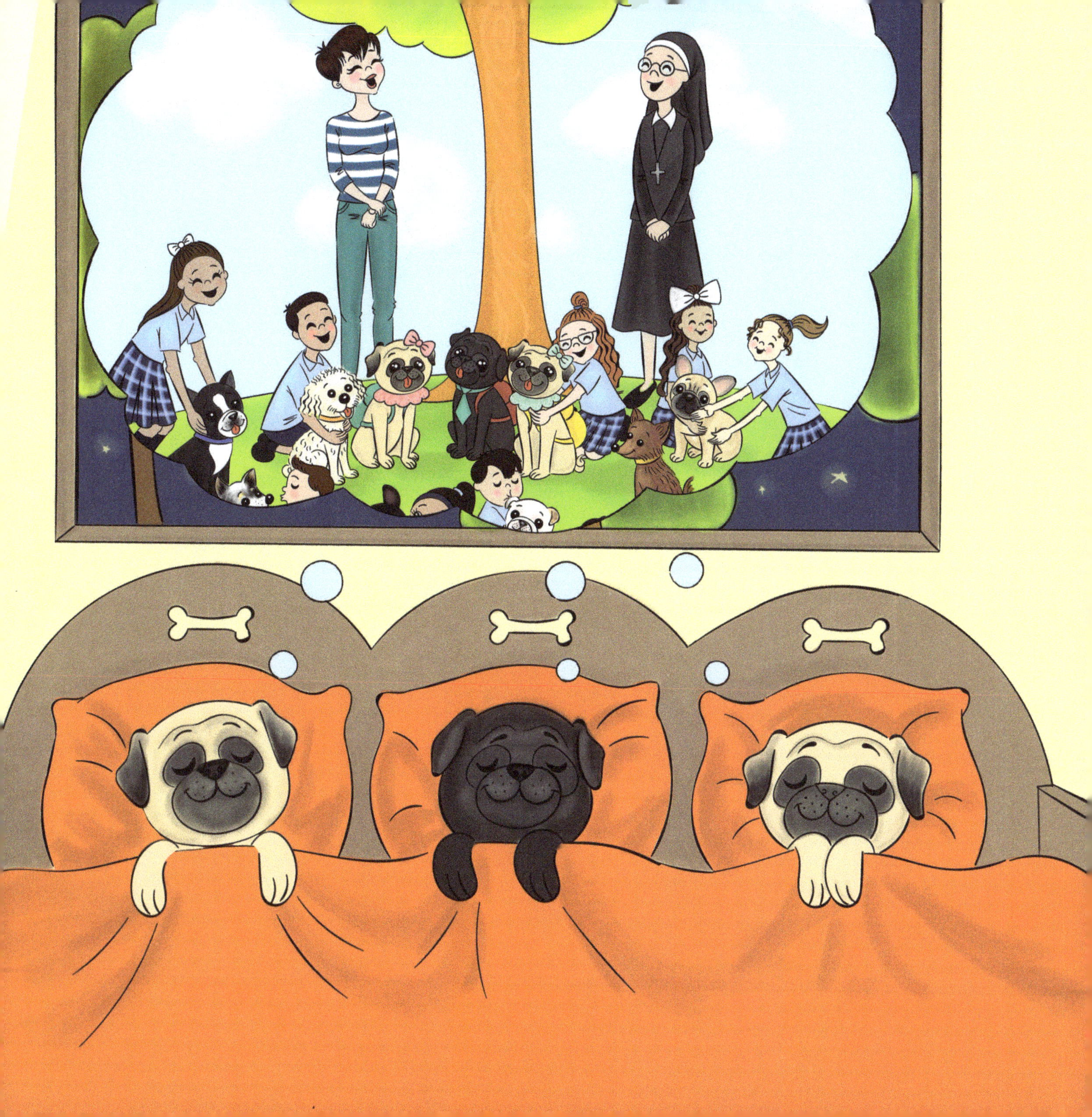

www.ingramcontent.com/pod-product-compliance
Lightning Source LLC
Chambersburg PA
CBHW061750290426
44108CB00028B/2950